SUSANNAH DICKEY is a poet and novelist from Derry and the author of four pamphlets, *I had some very slight concerns* (2017), *genuine human values* (2018), *bloodthirsty for marriage* (2020) and *Oh!* (2022). Her poems have been published in *The Poetry Review*, *The TLS*, *Poetry London*, and *Poetry Ireland Review*, amongst others. She is an Eric Gregory Award winner, a prize granted for a collection by poets under the age of thirty. Susannah is the author of two novels, *Tennis Lessons* (2020), and *Common Decency* (2022), both published by Doubleday UK and Penguin Ireland.

*Susannah Dickey*

# ISDAL

PICADOR

First published 2023 by Picador
an imprint of Pan Macmillan
The Smithson, 6 Briset Street, London EC1M 5NR
*EU representative:* Macmillan Publishers Ireland Ltd, 1st Floor,
The Liffey Trust Centre, 117–126 Sheriff Street Upper,
Dublin 1, D01 YC43
Associated companies throughout the world
www.panmacmillan.com

ISBN 978-1-0350-1505-4

1 3 5 7 9 8 6 4 2

A CIP catalogue record for this book is available from the British Library.

Printed and bound in Great Britain by TJ Books Ltd, Padstow, Cornwall

Visit **www.picador.com** to read more about all our books
and to buy them. You will also find features, author interviews and
news of any author events, and you can sign up for e-newsletters
so that you're always first to hear about our new releases.

[ ... ]

In November, 1970, a woman's body was found at Isdalen in Bergen,
Norway. Her status has been 'Unidentified' for __ years, __ months, __ days.
She was severely burnt on the front of her body (including her face and hair),
but not the back. The autopsy concluded that she died of a combination of
carbon monoxide poisoning (she wasn't dead at the time of burning) and a
barbiturate overdose. She has come to be known as the Isdal Woman.

# CONTENTS

# I – PODCAST

We can't be both pervert and detective.
— David Griffith

But Griffith is not right that we cannot be both pervert and detective.
— Maggie Nelson

## \* A gloomy introduction

When someone goes missing don't they usually go missed?
At the funeral there were no sandwiches, only solicited
seat fillers: policemen and out-of-work landscapers.

So, how did you know the deceased . . . ? The question tapers
because oops, nobody knew her. She gets buried in a zinc
-lined coffin, fresher than a BLT. The pianos plink.

\*

When they found her she looked like this (the silence of implied gesture).
Head down there, legs up there. Her visibly stopped internal esture.

\*

In a city on Norway's coast there's a grave untouched by lineage.
A single member's club with hidden entry and no signage.

# * More importantly!

Two podcast hosts captain the story's bounce and narrative thrust!
He's English! She's Norwegian! They need listeners to bestow their trust
and invest in this ten-part audio description of cruelty.
If ratings drop there's been a failure of either execution or loyalty.

# * Outtake #1

Try to postpone the conjuring of mental image until the sound
effects, he says. Not to be prescriptive but your inner eye's bound

to be more susceptible to assault without the tonic
of new info. We're already at a disadvantage through strictly sonic

conveyance. Not to go on about it, but when's the last time
someone you know was upset by simply hearing about a crime?

[4]

## * A spectacular funeral

The priest reads Proverbs verse 5 – he's upright and sonorous.
He tells the attendees: Drink from your own toilet before someone else's,
ship a water feature to someone beloved.

On his advisement, fathers go home to warn their sons: degloved
women aren't the answer. Marry the comely girls, predictable, well-fed.
Not the beautiful strangers, acicular and dead.

## * Some atmosphere-ing

Pine forests give way to scree and sunlight douses
the world for a few hours each afternoon, making empty houses
look lived in. (The silence of implied gesture.) Here it is, so many broken
trees. The earth wetter than what's hauled onto the banks of the Lofoten
or the last half inch in a Dijon jar. Welcome to Norway.
The weather's nice, at times. Have a nice stroll in the Ice Valley.

## * The triumph of scientific objectivity over faith

The hosts ingratiate themselves with listeners through anecdotal
story-telling and flirty repartee. They need the total
faith of their listenership. (Scurrying behind is the unpaid amanuensis.)
They must be likeable and reliable. The male host insists
the investigation is driven
by science. The female host says they've striven
for accuracy. Luckily, many advancements have been achieved
in science, she says. Forensics has come a long way since the 70s.


## * The pervasive nature of death

It's date night in Bergen. Isdal was found on Sunday
and all Sundays now feel less biblical, he says. You can pray
for stasis, but October conjures November, placeholder for a joyless

winter, she says. Outside are the members of the outrageous
tree gang: chestnut and spruce. Inside, by green-tinged candlelight,
their hands look molten and malachite.


## * Loosening corporeality

They follow valley lines to where she was found. It's not a well kerned
path but then, who would come here? It's neither church-turned-
restaurant nor ice rink, she says. The air's thick; it's giving them trouble.
We're part cloud (without the perks of being up or being soluble).

## *Isdalen, 1970, 29th November.
### Two girls go out with their father, a professor

(Professor Father.) With a brevity of light symptomatic of season
they forgo church to be frolicsome – sunlit heathens
in the valley. They need to find something
to do, so one girl finds a body. (Maybe she started calling
for her father. Maybe he caught up with her and held her
sister behind his back – already too late to save 50% of daughters
from seeing something troubling. Maybe he ignored intellectual impulse
and for the sake of appearances performed ineffectual pulse
checks on a body well past supple.) Like bikes in a velodrome,
they tilt back round the lake. He knocks on a door. He borrows a phone.

*

The first morning's headline read Young Girl Found Dead in Isdal.
(They didn't know her exact age but it's natural,
surely, to want to mourn a young girl.) The pugilist pose
of her itching body got immortalised in the attached, grainy photo
(although in it she's not so much girl as landscape and arrow
– maybe her father was a landscape, her mother an arrow).

[ 8 ]

*Upon merely seeing the colour red, the metabolic rate
of a human being increases by 13.4%*

The attendance, or lack thereof, of a fire at the crime scene
remains up for debate. The last living officer (winner of the tontine)
remembers evidence of one, but it transpires
the police reports don't mention it. Regardless: the body was on fire.

\*

When a person is burned the skin contracts: arms up, legs down.
She looked like the Fiji mermaid (or someone with abandon).

Her death stays open like an ending. Imagine the flush of Mary Hatch
with the stench of a blackened respiratory tract.

They can't rule out the possibility that this was a hard bitch. She ate
too many pills, the sort popular among dead women (barbiturates)

and reporters speculated suicide.
Easier ways to do it, though. (Silk chemise and water by the bedside.)

(For those who find description insufficient there's a shot
of the body online. It's black and white, but just imagine it's not.)

### * Outtake #2

The male host is worried the podcast form doesn't lend itself to shock.
The female host says if they garner enough interest (flock)
a better medium might take over, with inescapable visuals. (Chock)
The male host hopes their property rights will be respected. (Locke)
He's always wanted to see his name in white on a black screen. (Brock)

## * Dream of a postmortem

Her insides opening with the thick vapour of maraschino
acid. Her intestines are marinade sinister. Perhaps her uterus
looked like an attacked vine tomato. Lilting and neglected.
Hocked salsa and old potatoes.
How sordid is it to invent a reason to put hands in a woman?
No seriously, I'm asking. Look for the fatherly
chicken skin on her inner thighs – the parts the fire couldn't
mutate. Before she died an enemy fear must have leapt onto all
the different parts of her for them to catch in syllable-shaped
silver tins. A woman's debilitating unbelieved-ness infects
everything it touches. It must have been there on her burnt face
with winter and sabotage and misery and fabulous.
How unnecessary, perhaps, to kill a woman. So soft
but so un-mummed. So fabulous.

# * Production techniques

The hosts are intent on making the most compelling possible podcast.
The foley artist opens the door and invites in the neighbour's cat
and a hungry vampire. The rain starts and it's bubble wrap.
The rain falls and it's rice grains poured from burlap
onto chopping board. The rain gets heavier and it's a trapped
audience clapping behind a door. A small piano in an underpass
methodically tests the furthermost limits of its echoes.
Isdal wasn't shy – she had an agenda, a witness says on the next episode.

*

To solve interference, unscrew the back to find a set
of pursed lips expelling air with a noise like *pfftpopfft*.

Rub oil on the cracks and return the lid to the transistor
radio. A good-looking-sounding, teen-sounding chorister

goes Ooooh. It's possible Isdal was set alight then carried
up the mountain. The bottle of pills was recently emptied

– its contents rattling in her decommissioned stomach.
Around her were star fragments of petrol-soaked Cossack

hat. Trappings of Christmas, battlefield burial. Anyway, now this!
The hosts are off to the railway station with a crime novelist!

## * Inventory

In Bergen station the police found two suitcases.
They opened them, unaccustomed to a case like this.

What does a woman trying to change her looks look
like, in items? A postal service lingerie-branded matchbook,

a dirty fingerprint on the lens of a pair of sunglasses (no history
of canning pineapple). Next, a tonal inconsistency

with the naughty matchbook: a plastic bag from a family-owned
shoe shop. The underwear company eventually became a renowned

chain of sex shops, she says. Saucy, he says. Finally, the jig's
up on her feigning any sort of normal life: look at all these wigs!

What woman would have so many wigs! She's left these fripperies
for us to find! he says. Just look at this dead woman's proclivities!

## * New day, new episode

The sound of tunnelled cars. A bed sheet pulled across
a wooden floor. The sound of false memory then fog

horn. The hosts are aboard an ocean vessel.
The rain has taken its hard-earned sabbatical.

The archipelago is like knees and breasts as they break
the seal of bathwater. The archipelago is fungal hyphae

in a forgotten lunchbox. We're on the sun deck of an ocean
vessel, he says. In Stavanger you can't see a tree, even,

for fog. Stavanger is Norway's oil capital,
she says. It's pretty barren, he says. Isdal

went by boat, she says prettily. Our hairdos are messy,
he says. You look like you've got good sea legs, he says. Unless we

hit a rough patch, she says. To be a good Norwegian I must survive
this boat trip. He likes that she's open and less furtive

than Isdal. He looks at her sea legs and stops feeling queasy.
The valley music commences, becomes obelisk music. Alla breve.

The (redacted for ethical reasons) Hotel, Stavanger. Cashless
with uneven floors! Time for a testimonial from a receptionist
– an older lady with blonde hair and rubber
boots. She's in her 60s and her name sounds like tuna.
She's spent her life overwhelmed by the photo of the dystrophic
body. (The photo of the prostrate corpse.) She says, It was horrific.
Since then when I think about fires or people getting burned,
I see her. In 1970 she was 19 and hadn't yet learned
to recognise Soviet hats or teeth; hadn't begun to consider
how many of us are liable to die at the hands of some insidious other.
She knows better now though. She was suspicious of Isdal's credentials.
She sensed an agenda. The music crescendos.

*

The receptionist remembers Isdal's Vanessa
Paradis teeth and lisp and signature: the epée run through F and
the L like a bridal train. She was the only woman
staying by herself. She smelt of garlic and had a small room sans

en suite. The bellboy has info too! He remembers Isdal well, then
hesitates. He can't remember *exactly* but wow! – his first Belgian!
You never forget your first Belgian. Wow! A woman paying
attention to him! You don't forget a woman like that, is all he's saying.

He can't remember how the conversation started, or its exact nature
but he knows she couldn't say her S's properly (which made it even better).

[ 16 ]

## * The hosts do some contextual exposition

Easy to hide your identity, especially for someone so economical
with words as she, he says. It was easier to live an unchronicled
life in 1970, she says. The rain arrives like popcorn
hatching in a microwave. Bergen was sexy, then. Crop tops torn
shorter; mothers and women going to market to eye up debonair
sellers. There were demonstrations over long hair
and Vietnam. The girls' legs long with hot pants; the fjords tall
with submarines. Somehow things in 1970s Bergen were still cordial.
There was not yet an immediate threat to shake the firmament.
There was not yet the immediate threat of a hot engagement.

*

The colours of the houses by the port. Red from ochre
and animal oil (like her throat after carbon monoxide choked her).
Yellow from ochre and liver oil and white from zinc (like a coffin
– the remains therein just beginning to soften).

*

The female host admires his strict aesthetic tyranny.
The female host suspects that he couldn't define irony.

## *Sex sells

Today the podcast hosts are speculating about Isdal's lovers.
We're picturing them lining up to varnish her antiques over

a long weekend, he says. They're saying, Hey, whatcha thinking?
as they brush her hair behind her ear (belt buckles clinking).

They're maligning her weird accent and her poor elocution
but still wanting her. A woman couldn't stay in one location

for so long without having anyone, the hosts say. She's not an art
installation or a cold front. She'd depart

if she had no one – go elsewhere. They're inclined
to think there was a man. He must have lured her up the incline.

Did you know that 50%
of murdered women are murdered, a docent

tells them, by their partners, or ex-partners?
(The prospect of a woman dying single is a greater disheartener

than this fact, though.) When a woman is killed the police
should talk to the lovers, he says. Look, she says, look at the ice

-made divots. There are inlets from the sea formed by glaciers.
The amorous looks Isdal must have got, he says. The glacé cherries

of the female host's cheeks swell and he watches the cerulean
glass of her eyes. Maybe she's thinking about her own Vitruvian

lovers. How to understand a woman's thoughts? Their penumbra complexities. You can't. Onwards they go, into the tundra.

*

They repeat the year of her death as though it were ancient history. A corpse is under the jurisdiction of personal property rights, apparently.

# * A local driver speaks

A Stavanger taxi firm and another testimonial. He was called
for a pickup and there she was. How many legs did she have corralled
under that skirt? Just the right amount. Lips like an instrument
and ass like an instrument. Sexy body with hips like a church to foment
internal unrest. A gap between her teeth. Who could pretend
to care about the shrubs arguing on doorsteps or the drowned
fish being wheeled into town? He describes her with unveiled alacrity.
Did he mention her tooth gap? God, she was pretty.

*

They're in an evidence locker. A Norwegian voice is dubbed
with Lazenby or private school. He'll risk his life to get up

on a chair to reach this shelf. He retrieves a bag of saved
jaws. We only keep the unclaimed jaws, he says. A claimed

jaw's worthless. DON'T THROW AWAY MEDIEVAL SKULL
a label says. There's a noise like a mousetrap, or opposable

thumbs in a sack, tap dancing. He'll bet
his life to make this jaw laugh like a castanet!

No but really, he doesn't mean to be disrespectful. He says sorry
to the ceiling. The small piano is wheeled into a hospital foyer

with a film crew. 134 / 70 is the reference for her mandible.
He presents it to the hosts. Here it is, postprandial,

ad summum. There'll be good-looking women regardless
of this, but she'll be under earth with her skull jawless

in its lower half, flaccid like a foxglove or a Jacobean.
Even like this, in its acid-dried state, lithic as cuttlebone,

you can imagine the wetness of her mouth. A pale mist
coating her tongue in case someone inserted a fist.

## * Ekphrasis after fingerprints

This is a woman who's never canned pineapple for a living.
Right thumb is a man shoehorned into a cave instructed
to think of the consequences of things he'll never experience
first hand. Right index is a right breast mashed flat
against a shower door as she gets taken
roughly from behind. (It's hard to know if we want this woman
to have been taken.) Right middle is a smooth surface split
open the emerging fractals observed from above. There was once a tree
performing a reverse kerb stomp in a suburb. Undoing years
of industry tarmac and gravel. Made you think about who was there
first. Updigging it was like excising a two-hander tumour wrapped
around a spinal cord. Made you wonder if it was worth the effort.
Anyway, that's right middle. Left index and right middle were once
inseparable. The last time they spoke one said Remember when?
and the other said Vaguely. Left thumb is salmon done
with fresh lemon and left ring is just what it is: a fingerprint.
A reminder this woman once held a suitcase like she had somewhere
to go and would get to. The rest are extras: petalled faces in a crowd.
Left little is the same man from the cave again. Bowing first
to circumstance and then looking up. Wondering just
when it is that a sky and a ceiling cease to be different.

## * Peripatetic in more ways than one!

The 1940s loosen her wet-fingered scrambling for arête.
The hosts have her hostel registration documents. She was not yet
30 when she died, apparently! She wrote her birth year as '43, '42, '45.
She was young! he says. On one doc her next stay was Trondheim,
her previous stay Brussels. On another her next stay Oslo,
her previous London. It can't all be true. It gives us pause, though.

*

The hosts are tired. I love Spain, he says. Welcome to Spain,
she says. It'll be nice to see her out from under all those plain

and dowdy layers. She arrives late. Problems with the plane,
she says, with the ice – it was stuck fast like galium aparine.

They had to chip away at it. I couldn't get here soon
enough. Now they're between blues (Hockney macaroon).

The sky licking heads and stretches of Mediterranean playa
and a cloudless sea. They can see Marbella

from here. How's my pronunciation?
he says, attempting a Nordic phrase. Your enunciation

is a bit off, she says. She's all new wife-y in her holiday t-shirt.
The voice in the Sat Nav is a woman's voice. She shirks

her responsibilities and forgets an exit but
they forgive her. She sounds excited,

he says. They're going to visit a crime reporter. Y
donde ahora? he asks the Sat Nav. (Escape that pathetic fallacy!)

The foley artist rustles a crisp multipack to find a flavour,
or it's a crinoline skirt, or a dog's ear bitten for bad behaviour.

The hosts are performing an inventory of things still
held, and things now lost. They have her jaw – her mouth was filled

with gold. She had slippers printed with the word Italy, and eczema
cream. She had another bag from another shoe shop. Roma,

the bag says. She had 500 deutschmarks and a Norway road map.
She had a sewing kit and a steel spoon and a compass.

## * Expert input from a dentist

She had teeth extracted early in her life, compensated
for with belated dental treatment. Lucky she wasn't cremated.

*

It's been lovely to read your theories and your responses
in the Facebook group. Let's take a moment to thank our
sponsors.

# * Cold war spy with a mouth full of gold fillings

This is what she was after: a big light-eating slice of butternut squash
for a mandible. When people offer you a slice of the action the action
is surely squash-coloured. If you've been a girl during the period
of (still as-yet undetermined boundaries) you've been taught to want legs
like Fran Kubelik or the green M&M. Feet the shape

of seal pups without shoes and enough gold to fill a bath. When she goes
to the dentist he shows her his ampoules all full up with soft lighting.
He asks her if she's ready to be mouth-rich mouth-coronal.
She says Yes please make me top-heavy epinasty. Everyone's worried
about their tits – if their blue-green-edged buoyancy is even

reliable. She's been holding hers in the bath like she's Mary II
at coronation. She's never wanted to be a role model. Who has time?
In the dentist she's hooked herself a man who likes colours not words
and she's got big gums full of gold. Would you just look at her.
Sexy legs jusqu'au soleil! Hole in her face like Kremnica!

## * Outtake #3

To be a woman and interested (in an anthropologically
detached way) in another woman's murder isn't subversive
anymore. It's as brave as eating
battery farmed chicken or setting fire to a crash test dummy.
If a thing's very purpose is suffering it isn't radical
to enjoy inflicting violence upon it.
But wait – the study of canonical violence
isn't the same as the infliction of violence.
But looking at an act isn't the same as studying it.
And witnessing an act isn't the same as committing it.
So, I guess we're at an impasse.
Somewhere between depravity and righteousness.
And where's that?
The recent market demand for velodromes,
I suppose. We can edit this later. Throw in some xylophones.

The hosts are interviewing staff in one of the final hotels.
Amazing how many people rush to offer testimonials.

He's picturing Isdal's glamour and olive skin; fine clothing
and brown eyes; the smell of garlic. She's always moving

from hotel to hotel then finally to the Hotel Hordeheimen
(redact it!) on secret business. She was surely involved in crime and

/ or espionage. On the fourth-floor corner is the last room
she ever lived in. The current staff know second-hand her perfume,

but nobody mentions garlic. This time she was spicy
and her handwriting erratic. Her disguise

was slipping, he says, she was attracting attention. Her ermine,
her allure – not very inconspicuous. His voice fades to a theremin.

In the hotel (redacted for ethical [ . . . ]) – Wait, did we redact it?
– Isdal is rearranging the furniture. We've collected

several testimonials, he says. When she was in the room
she moved the armchair to the corridor, it would reassume

its proper place only when she went out. That's how the staff
knew they could sneak in with towels. (A professional gaffe

to do so.) Soon after, she was found. Although found implies
looking. Soon after, she was seen. By then, she wasn't alive.

*When the armchair was out she was in when the*
*armchair was in she was out*

*The armchair 1*

The armchair has convinced her that someone's watching
not just where she is, but where she's going to be. On checking
in she put a necklace on and accosted the armchair.
She did the invisible high jump and landed and dust hissed
      anaerobic a roman candle.

*The armchair 2*

Get all up in me little girl, it said and she felt like an egg
in a slipper. It feels like a gift from a mother it feels like insight.
The armchair is indented with all the places old feelings
have happened. Through the window she can see one end
      of the street to the other.

*The armchair 3*

The ground outside is cholesterol. She likes to think of herself
safe as a chocolate chip in mint green exterior.
She sits perpendicular to the armchair on the armchair
like she's the armchair's subtitle. Or like it is a gymnast in lycra
      and she is a gymnast in lycra.

*The armchair 4*

The hypethral circus of morning has yellow and lilac and griffins.
The armchair questions the general lack of consistency
in her personality. It tells her she's good looking like a mistress.
She puts on perfume. Get spicy for me, the armchair says,
      I want you to smell like good morals.

*The armchair 5*

The armchair says, Those towels look different from before.
She says, Do they? They look at the towels for a bit
and the armchair says, Don't they? She wishes it would leave her
to her rubber boots. It says, You can't go outside until they switch
        the night back on.

*The armchair 6*

In the morning it says, I hope Madame will be buying the not
included breakfast. She has tomatoes and cigarettes.
The armchair welcomes her back. It encourages her to support
local businesses and at least in this she can't question the ratio
        of people to people who would miss her.

*The armchair 7*

The armchair wakes her like a forgotten birthday. Her head
protrudes from the duvet. She's the long straw in a fistful
of short straws. If she could get her hands on two ends
        she'd make them kiss like Barbies.
If she could lead herself to fire, she wouldn't waste the breath.

*The armchair 8*

She dreams about taking the armchair to a beauty spot and picking
up an onion-sized rock. She pictures going. Her urges never looked
so big or dangerous. She hoists the armchair like a catfish and sets it
in the hall. It calls to her. It says, Elozabith Eluzibath
        did you actually think you'd be safe now?

## * History

In the 60s and 70s the Russians were watching a penguin
closely off the coast of Norway. The Norwegians were sanguine

about the missile's prospects. In the secret police archive
her file is dateless, marked SECRET. (No use for the ablative

case.) SECRET is the second highest classification apparently.
(The highest classification is a secret.) It's a thin file, they soon see,

but it does have one good document. It broaches the universal
topic of a local fisherman. (Isdal managing to ensorcell

any man who saw her.) How could he resist the urge to get near
her? She was watching missile tests by the water like it was New Year.

## * Penguin / Fat goose

A funny name for devastating weapons
(did you know an alternative Germanic word is Fettgans?).

*

The hosts have dinner by the flippy flame of a tealight.
They discuss their childhoods. His fingers cast spatulate

shadows. He says, Did you see periscopes in the fjords
growing up? No, she says, but we were taught fear, to hoard

food and water. He's imagining her young, with looks like an au pair.
She's imagining Russians, sneaking into the water like copper.

## * *The fisherman is long dead,*
## *but God bless primogeniture*

Crime is not the prerogative of the air borne. (Or more
accurately, crime is the concern of the earth-bound.) A core
witness offers new information. The *son* of the fisherman.

A man of few words (his primary words were Chondrichthyan
and Osteichthyes) took his young family to the train station.
The police gifted him three things: a caution

about personal safety, a knife, and a gun.
They spent their Christmas (with gun and knife) in London
and sometimes he glanced, and for a long time would glance,

over his shoulder for dangers against which he stood no chance
of protecting them (even with knife and gun). Overhead, the sundry
birds confabbed (Teach a man to fish and he'll never go hungry.

Give a man a gun and he'll never need protection.) about the anger
that necrotises in the years after a mistake, that bores like an auger
in the years following the admission of dangerous knowledge.

Is honesty the best? He endangered his family for the sake of adage.

*Interview with the son of the now-dead fisherman*
*(the summer the fish arrived in the net pre-cooked)*

The last memory anyone has of the fisherman is of a man shape
by the evening quayside. Of how blue will always expand to fill
its container. Of him saying, I've been inside so long I've forgotten
how to wear a hat. Before he died the fisherman liked to speak

about a woman he saw once. He'd just got a new trawler.
It was difficult to evenly distribute his attention. The woman looked
Slavic and the same could not be said of his trawler. She was nice,
for someone not talking to him. Sometimes the sky's a bed

sheet and sometimes it's pavlova. Sometimes it's a reminder
you've been awake too long. When I got a fire escape it was better
than a bicycle, he might have heard her say. Better than a hundred
bicycles. There were wet leaf moments watching the precursor

of light shrink like old skin. When a plane went over and I pretended
it was my pet. The convex acne of metal putting dents in my sole.
The fisherman might have heard all this and more. Maybe he decided
he wanted a summer with a title. The Summer We Broke

Our Back Teeth On A Bottle Cap. Why have an exit route
be so hospitable? maybe he heard her say. I wanted to stay there till I got hot.

## * A potted history of spy activity within Norway

A nurse retrained to retain her boyfriend. He smelled of nefarious
past, recent imprisonment, fish. She smelled of rod of Asclepius,

a Bodø hospital, virtue. She died in prison facing charges of treason.
(Norwegian women love the smell of honey in a trap.) The lesson

is that ladies are easily seduced into the sink. The harder to précis,
more confusing lesson is the ouroboros of it all: women shouldn't be

allowed to become spies. They fall in love and become spies.
Women shouldn't be allowed to become spies. They fall in love
and become spies. Women shouldn't be allowed to become
spies. They fall [ . . . ]

Anyway, we digress. Luckily someone was hired to enliven
the info: *www.dagbladet.no/magasinet/sjarmert-til-spionasje/65961967*

## * Digression #1

He offers her some lasagna. She smiles and says, Yes.
He says, I hope our podcast passes the béchamel test.

# * On to the good stuff

Time for the interview with a spy catcher (after much preparatory
bureaucracy). They've sought him out for a priori

speculations about spy behaviour. She's been trying for two years
to get this interview. The listeners only get to hear

of this now the two years is over. (Ignorance of happenings
is the same as nothing happening.) Is spy catcher a kenning?

he asks. Yes, she says, for a comically oversized butterfly net.
They've arrived at a bungalow-d and diffident

cul-de-sac. There's a key in a lock and a jocular Hi
in Norwegian. The listeners are wondering if a joke's implied,

but at whose expense? The door opens and a tall man, audibly
in his 90s, stoops. The male host calls his blue eyes laudable.

It's no exaggeration to call these eyes the most piercing
in existence, he says. I can only imagine them searing

into you over a long interrogation. Nobody has a response.
Nice area, someone says. The hosts hold hands like it's a séance.

(The sound of implied gesture.) A murmuration wrings
in a blender. To sound, whatever trompe l'oeil is to all things

visible. The male host eyes the man's priapic
cane. Here's someone who knows their spies. A little dactylic —

the echo of cane on the tiles. (A gong gets struck
in the opposite of an anechoic

chamber.) What is the opposite? he asks. A soup tureen,
she says. Struck hard enough to dislodge its patina of gangrene.

## *Transcript of the interview with a spy catcher (hairspray monologue)*

Keep your adulation and your muffins. He's at saturation
point which is a euphemism for being near completion –
for having nearly finished living well. He ought not to have been
called to the scene at all. You don't invite a palaeontologist
to a Sylvanian families convention or a forester to a bird bath.
Asked about the possible presence of espionage he says: Nothing
more potentially fatal for women than women's vanity.
Then: I told the chief of police it was no case of murder.
Keep your reveries and your orisons and your vol-au-vents.
Everywhere she went she was seen to have a massive can
of hairspray. Wherever she was on the street she had a massive can
of hairspray in her hand. Unimportant little woman set herself alight.
He says: Intelligence murders were done with knives and guns
and poison, not burning. Listen: the desired retention of beauty
is more rapacious than the desired acquisition of beauty.
Listen: This is my reverie: there was only as much her as there was
the most recent thought of her held by anyone. She was only ever
as young as she was in her today, she was only ever as beautiful
as she was at her most recent. Women are obsolescent
and they hate it, he says. A cake forgotten about only liked
for the making a long walk started in olding sunlight
a rotting horizon abortive wants a poinsettia bought pre-potted
then not looked at till Tuesday's disappointment.
FUCKING APPLES. But I digress. Anyway: she dropped the can
into the fire and caught fire, and as for her eight identities,
that's not my concern. I've done my appraisals and I'll be dead soon.
Keep your new evidence and your tectonic biscuits.
Where I'm going, I'll have no use for loose ends.

The spy catcher has closing remarks. He says, The classic MO is
to destroy the paper with your instructions. You memorise

it, then eat it. The gong's doing arias now. They percolate
through a grid. Good spies eat paper. That's just how they operate.

## * The hosts ruminate over their professional manifesto

What they'd like is a subscription to their depiction
of bodily vulnerability, followed by some mild protestation,

followed by acquiescence, followed by an acceptance of sorts.
They can't get her consent, so in its place they'll take yours.

*

The sound of time travel, or flashback. Not travel. Reversal.
A whispering tree and a microphone imitating a pipistrelle.

Smack smack. It wasn't the tree whispering, it was the woman inside
the tree. Go into the body. Find tissues: proteins and peptides.

Ears, the hair, the teeth, can all tell us things. The body interred
has no jaw because we have it, he says. On the enamel find sulphur,

carbon, strontium. Your teeth know where you were, such
is their purview. If questioned they'll give it up willingly. A Dutch

isotope expert sees himself as astrophysicist, chemist, physicist.
He says he understands the universe. No one's more equipped

to understand what we're made of. He does his best to sequester
her. She began in South Germany then moved west then wester

to Belgium, France, Spain. Across the channel to Wales. Landscape
music starts – the sound of dynamism. Fog horns adumbrate.

*A spy turned writer turned historian is also sceptical of Isdal's credentials*

Let me tell you, he says, A Soviet spy in the field wouldn't smell

of garlic. She'd smell sexy; she'd smell of Chanel No. 5.
She wouldn't reveal herself as foreign; it would thwart her
motive.

Another thing: there were very few female KGB
spies. (Women shouldn't be allowed to become . . . ) C'est la vie,

the male host says. (The palindromic hoo ooh of the vocalist.
The palindromic aah haa of the strings.) The off-piste

nature of Isdal is cause for curiosity, he says. This germinates
a new enquiry: does the female host wear Chanel? She obviates

the question. They gesture flirtatiously to statistical impossibility.
She is implicitly fragrant. A dulcimer plings languidly.

A mirror on the ceiling to check how you look to the approaching
rain. (Chandelier to rain what photo is to life.) A rapprochement

with an irked maître d' who remembers Isdal's coming to dine.
At every meal her eyes were wet. Saline

-filled eyes. There was a man with her (at last our perverse
desire for man is vindicated!), with whom she never conversed.

They sat in silence. It was unromantic, unfamiliar.
(The sound of a man's voice blubbing. His phonetic milieu

is among other bubbles inarticulate.) Nobody fails
to recall Isdal. She made an impression. The maître d' paled

at even sitting on the same chair as her. The female host wagers
he might have thought murder contagious.

## *Maybe Isdal was trying to block the door

A dead chambermaid gave intel prior to expiry.
Back then the room had a narthex by the door – a foyer

where the table sat sometimes. Isdal had a turquoise
bath robe that she wore through the halls. (No choice

of an en suite back then.) A turquoise robe is so lissom
an item to drape over fear. Flimsy like delphiniums.

*When the table was out and upside down she was in
when the table was in and right way up she was out*

*The table 1*

This bloody woman. Moving the furniture again.

*The table 2*

It's so often the case, isn't it Eluzabith? If a man wants
to hurt you a table in a hallway won't do much good.

*The table 3*

A chambermaid presses down her cuticles in wait.
She tugs a swan through the halls by its neck.
(A hoover made of life.)

\*

(The sound of muffled squabbles intimate intimate dischord.)
Isdal and a man bought a mirror from a homeware store.

Wall-mounted and cheap, the then-young retail worker (now old)
describes it to the hosts. Nobody could have foretold

the mirror's tragic brevity of use. Why buy a mirror
when staying in a hotel? the hosts ask. She paid more

attention to how she looked than was normal – she had creams
and wigs and a mirror too big for her handbag. She seems

to have been attracting attention, which isn't spy behaviour
– you'd keep a low profile. Her hair this time was curlier

than usual (A wig! WIG!). On November 19th she was Elizabeth.
Penultimate hotel and ultimate pseudonym before death.

\*

One night a maid entered to undress the beds for evening,
but Isdal was in there. The maid thought about leaving,

but didn't. A man was there too, procacious
on a small couch. The maid waited for them to be gracious

about her intrusion but instead
they said nothing. Isdal had such specific eyes (credited

for their sadness) and a black dress. The maid apologised
for not knocking. They rhapsodised

silence. The maid described the man as 25–30. Nice face. Grey suit.
(Various different witnesses describe him as hirsute

– either blonde or grey.) He was possibly two different men,
which would fit the hosts' idea of her (long rid of her hymen!).

Regardless, the police never tried to find him / them.
(Isdal and he argued in the homeware store but not in German

or English.) The police never sought out the bellicose
man / men. Their attention stayed on Isdal – her smelly clothes

and diastema. The following night she faced a dilemma, moved to a hotel
across the harbour. (The sound of tourmaline pan pipes and tubular bell.)

The hosts think she wanted a window from which she could spectate.
On the Facebook group there's been speculation of late

about the underwear company matchbook: was she a prostitute?
The female host thinks no. Mere underwear doesn't constitute

professionalism. It's not sexy enough, she says, reluctant to placate
them. A suitcase of normal underwear does not a prostitute make.

And why would she check into Christian hotels? he says. (The Venn
diagram of sex work and God is a bicycle.) The Hordeheimen

and the Neptune wouldn't have permitted her to ply her trade.
It's better that she's not a prostitute. (More sympathy to aggregate.)

(It's a fine line we're treading, somewhere between fetishistic
dispassion and empathy. We want hungry listeners (not sexist

ones).) But we're starting to digress, she says. Time to pack it
in for the night. (Oops, the hotel names should have been redacted.)

* Digression #2

Hordeheimen's a funny name, he says, Bit salacious.
He's hoping for a laugh, but she isn't impressed by facetious
paronomasia (especially when it ridicules her native language).
He offers her some apology lasagna from the mini fridge.

## * Time for a demotion

The former spy looks at her route. He thinks she was a courier
passing info to a handler. Sound the theory alarm (a cor anglais).

It's a theory! the male host shouts. An espionage ring,
the former spy suspects. She was involved with high-ranking

officials, the former spy suspects. She was a courier and they killed
her,
the former spy suspects. In this business professional error

will cost you, the former spy shrugs (the silence of implied gesture).
It's high stakes, the spy business: infiltration and purpresture.

## * *Now back to some science*

Your age is written in your mouth. Now imagine
this: a woman writing her aspirational age in
ink on her back tooth, as a means of evading demise.
A bit like wanting the bullet with your name on – to galvanise
your string against the Moirai's scissors. Maybe the tooth alongside
that one said CYANIDE
CAPSULE, with an arrow. Some kind of pis aller.
(She remains an anonymous notch on the tally.)


## * *Now back to some science*

More double bass. Numna numna. A handwriting expert at Kripos
is looking at the hotel documents: at the forceful riposte
of the crossbars Isdal drew on her F's and her T's.
This doesn't look like Norwegian handwriting to me,
the expert says. Different countries use different copybooks in schools
and the crossbar of her T might as well be a reticle
in how it betrays her. She learned to write in French
in a French speaking country. The isotope tests
told us she started life in Eastern Germany.
What prompted the move West? What insurgency
could have driven her to the border?

(Little by little they're unravelling her mystery's disorder.)

## * They're desperate to know her age

The sound of a drill. Hitchcock bathroom music. Then a scientist
cutting into tooth to determine the presence in her environment

of carbon-14. If she was born in the 40s it'll be in the teeth
that lurked under-gum while bombs detonated from 1955–63.

(The silence of implied suspense.) But it's not there. What perfidy
is this? he says. She *lied* about her age! I don't feel betrayed per se,

I just wonder would we even be here had we known this before.
Trousselier lantern music: the music of narrative dolour.

## * Isotope disappointment

It transpires she was not not yet thirty!
She was over forty and her childhood was the property
of the years between wars. Those mephitic
years yielded this not-young woman, who kept her age hermetic-
ally sealed till now. This changes the whole picture! Her mise-
en-scene frays and their narrative becomes contrived. Why tell lies
about your age if not to appeal to men? he asks. Maybe it raised
fewer questions about her travelling by herself,
she says. After all: a 45-year-old woman ought not to be
on the shelf.

## * A Hail Mary maybe

But wait: a new avenue presents itself. Now her true age
is known they can better situate her frieze! They triage
her characteristics by anticipated listenership appeal,
and perform, with a flourish, the big reveal:

20s Nuremberg! Quick, cue the cacophony . . .
this was the cradle of Nazi philosophy!

Lighthouse music gives way to Hitler noise. Plaintive
child soprano and archive marching. In lieu of young, they'd give
*anything* for her to be Jewish. There'd be sympathy
and intrigue, if only she were Jewish! The timpani
commence. (The silence of implied hope.) Rally music, applause,
rain. Rain then birds. Birds triumphant on rain, rain lawless
on birds. A night flight to Nuremberg (prescribed by the isotope map).
There's not much out the window (just Diet Coke black).

## *Take this time to reflect on what we've described

the audible handling of siphoned yolk and spilt yoghurt to be marrow and lymph the pursed lips of sulking interns by half-filled jugs to capture the gooseness of wind in a haunted forest three choristers at varying stages of sexual maturity to be sylph then nymph the specific silence of cuckoo's spit can be done with fairy liquid on a piglet's ear various ways of achieving rain cous cous into a stainless steel sink coffee granules palmed over the brink of a kitchen counter onto linoleum flooring grain poured into a car windshield pasta for hail fusilli for spring hail penne for November a shower left running behind a locked bathroom door walnuts into a bowl with varying degrees of reticence depending on the hunger of the interns a half deck of cards shuffled by trained fingers a quick played game of pelmanism flip book of paper that was soaked and then dried a television with a broken aerial left on pulling weeds from waterlogged soil is the same as a person struggling up a hillside intent makes little difference to sound fraying rope rubbed between hands is good for sinister in the absence of rope use hair in the absence of hair use air air rubbed at high velocity between dry palms is a bird taking off rubber gloves and flapping them is the realistic sound of bird wings fill a leather pouch with corn starch and crunch it for feet on snow walk through snow on all fours for a slow mouth masticating cruciferous vegetables roll up a phone book and hit an intern with it for an authentic simulation of inflicted violence if cellulite had a sound it would be tofu mashed with a fork for torpedoes it is silence followed by the opposite of silence to create silence rustle foil with fingers to create torpor or fire rustle foil with fingers ask the interns to acquire ageing furniture for the simulation of interviews conducted with world weary individuals for a brain haemorrhage squeeze a used teabag till the purse of pressure-induced perforation happens and if it sounds nothing like a haemorrhage then it's due to an unfamiliarity with the soft-spoken marram of thoughts leaking for seagulls pull catguts across an untuned viola for a heart rate accelerating before stoppage entirely misuse an ageing tumble dryer

## * Inconclusive

The hosts are grumpy. (The answers they sought, proven
fetter.) Honestly? The less said about the excursion
the better.


## * She's not Jewish, a summary:

- A chapel, turned foster home in 1928.
- A cardboard file in the basement reads 'Hitler Zeit'.
- The male host corrects a German preacher's pronunciation.
- It could be there were children there from Bavaria. Some
of whom could have been Jewish? the host asks. Unlikely,
an expert on the area's history says. A glockenspiel lazily
dings another dead end. Plenty of reasons to leave Nuremberg,
and without a name they can't trace her to the Maria Rosenberg
School.

Regardless, maybe a disrupted
childhood could have led to espionage, especially once
the Cold War
erupted?

\*

Orphans have the seeds sown early for different identities.
(The hosts take a moment to thank those who designed the websites.)

## * Things are drying up

The hosts have dinner. It's the last episode and a question mark hangs
over the unmarked grave. Sparking sounds of hazelnuts Petrarchan
in their pans. The hillside outside Bergen has become ferrous
in its magnetism. The path is now well-marked with Ferris
wheels, busy with roast hazelnut stalls. Corpse found in landscape
becomes landscape. Landscape becomes her. People traipse
from all over to see the landmark of Isdal. Has she got under your skin?
he wants to know. Croquettes glisten assonantly. She's been living
with Isdal for longer than he has, after all. I stayed in a hotel in Soho
recently, she says. Her graceful throat glows. The Debussy oboe
trills on grace notes. It was one of those rooms that seems in thrall
to time. It spooked me. Were you tempted to put the desk in the hall?
he says. They laugh good-naturedly (a will-they-won't-they bonhomie).
She says, No, but my boss suggested I sit down and write some poetry.

## * Outtake #4

You're really upset by all this, aren't you? he wants to know.
(Miss it / dismiss it)
If I were, what would that mean for what we've done? she says.
(Complicit)


## * Outtake #5

The flashes of insight that come in poetry can't absolve
us of our ignorance, she says.
Did you come up with that? he says, It's amazing.
No, it was someone else, she says. I'm just paraphrasing.

## *One last piece of evidence (make it quick)

The spoon. Also inside the case was a spoon with an engraving!
What significance had it for the woman in the grave in
rainy Bergen, under the rhododendron bush? A cursory
Google takes them to the Peerist Catholics. The order is sorry
to say they know nothing about cutlery. Strange to carry a Catholic
spoon if she was Jewish, she says. (This apostolic
possibility thwarts their last, lingering hopes.) She also carried a Madonna
and child picture, he says, But then, we know her to have donned a
disguise or two. Maybe these were just part of it. (The chorister is older
now – no longer coquette.) Turns out the inscription is just a soldered
on trademark for an Austrian steel company: Schütz & Patry.

thus, the last lead dries up. This is it: end of the party.

*The hosts go back to their lives largely unscathed*

Her final moments escape their domain. They've failed to get to the truth
of her. They'd like to thank the Facebook group: every amateur sleuth.

They've done their best to extrapolate her chronology,
but hers is a death ill-suited to big broadcast-funded hauntology.

*

All of this is ultimately speculative. They hope most of it is right.
At the airport the silence of gesture follows each to their respective flight.

The science of conjecture is never an exact one – loose ends
unavoidable. The listenership wonders if they were ever really friends.

## * Outtake #6

You can't spell Isdal
without I

the girl (now woman)
who found her says.

You can't spell Isdal
without is

the female host (briefly concerned
with temporality) says.

You can't spell Isdal
without laid

the male host says.

What?

the women say.

What?

the male host says.

## * Outtake #7

Isdal all there is?

the male host says.

Time doesn't always
condone levity

the female host says.

## * Outtake #8

Can it be voyeurism if she's already dead?
I don't know.
But.
What?
In recruiting this harem of voyeurs we've diverted them from –
From what?

## * Outtake #9

If anyone finds this perverse, they can just return to it later.
Later they'll be bound to find it excoriating and clever.

## * Outtake #10

I think we've fixed something here.
What?
Entertainment, maybe? Women? Whatever it is, we've fixed it.

# II – NARRATIVE

To remain with the dead is to abandon them.

— Anne Michaels

Was Princess Diana ever really alive? I mean, alive
to
anyone outside of her friends and family – truly?

— Claudia Rankine

[ · · · ]

In the grainy photograph of her body, she looks like a toppled, wind-beaten caryatid; as though she were never alive, or rather, as though the life that she had was one of stasis – an entity launched to its maximum functionality, optimum beauty, since undone by time.

When a person's notoriety stems from their death, they seem to have a different type of biographical topography. They're known for their death, so this might as well be their birth. Their existence is concomitant with their no longer existing, a singular point around which the circumstances and ephemera of their life and death orbit. It's not life as line but life as dot with encircling matter.

[ ... ]

I see a tweet from a stranger that says:
> 'Necrophilia is only "wrong" in so far as it is a violation of personal
> property right (the family owning the corpse as personal property) which
> makes it a lot less "immoral" (whatever that is) than people think.'

The necessity, or supposed necessity, of the tweet requires two assumptions:
one, that people are getting unduly outraged about necrophilia, and two, that
people *can* be unduly outraged about necrophilia.

The tweet is assuming a lot, in terms of how it frames the body. It makes of
the body a kind of vessel or vehicle, briefly utilised in the service of living,
eventually left vacant. To be thought of, really, with no more deference than a
microwave. If this is how we think of bodies, what makes any assault on any
body, occupied or otherwise, different from property damage? I spend some
time thinking about it, and I am confident the general populace does not agree
with Mr. Necrophilia Apologist, not least because if that were the case, I can't
imagine we would be so obsessed with dead bodies.

[ ... ]

We can't get enough of dead bodies, women's especially.

Elisabeth Bronfen writes, 'Because they are so familiar, so evident, we are culturally blind to the ubiquity of representations of feminine death.'

[ . . . ]

After listening to the podcast about the Isdal Woman, and after visiting the Facebook page where amateur detectives posit theories, I start wondering about True Crime.

For a death to be worthy of the True Crime treatment, it seems to require two avenues of potential exploitation: one, that the victim be intriguing, and two, that there be sufficient inconclusivity around their death as to permit rampant speculation.

For a person to garner sympathy from us, they must be made to be like us. To garner fascination, they must be made to be unlike us. For pathos the first is needed, for perversion the second. Regardless of whether the desired elicitation is one, or both, it's an act of making. Formulating theories about their death is equally an act of making.

[ · · · ]

In *The Topeka School*, by Ben Lerner, much is made of the thematic apperception test, or the TAT. 'Now I am going to show you a picture and I'd like you to make up a story about it. A story with a beginning, a middle, and an end.'

In an early episode of the podcast, the hosts describe (limited by their non-visual format) the photograph of the Isdal Woman's body. Listeners are invited to go online and look at it for themselves.

'What are the people in this picture thinking? Feeling? Start by telling me what led up to this scene.'

[ · · · ]

In *A Practical Guide to the Thematic Apperception Test*, the test is said to 'provide essentially idiographic rather than nomothetic information.' The test 'is quite effective in telling the clinician how the subject views the self and the world in his or her unique way.' The test is fundamentally an exercise in narrativisation.

[ . . . ]

In 1944, psychologists Fritz Heider and Marianne Simmel conducted a study. They made a short, animated film – about 2 ½ minutes long. In the film, three geometric figures (a large triangle, a small triangle, and a circle) move in various directions, at various speeds. They interact with a large rectangle, a section of which can open and close, as a door does. The film was shown to three groups of undergraduate students, who were then asked questions of varying ambiguity. The first experiment kept instructions general ('write down what happened in the picture') and the latter two experiments asked questions of greater specificity while also, in the case of the third experiment, showing the film in reverse. Although the TAT is never explicitly mentioned in the study, this investigation into the 'psychology of perception' seems a natural participant in the history of projective techniques.

Da Vinci:
> 'Don't take my advice lightly when I advise you, even though it may appear boring to stop and gaze at wall spots, or at the ashes in the fire, in the clouds, or in the mud and at similar things; you will, if you consider it carefully, discover in it many wonderful things.'

[ . . . ]

Although the introduction to *A Practical Guide* says the test reveals idiographic, rather than nomothetic information, the results of the Heider-Simmel study betray consistencies within individual narrative impulses. 50% of the responses to the film suggest that the two triangles are men, who fight over the woman, the circle. When asked what was happening when the big triangle and the circle were in the house together, 75% of the responses cast the big triangle as the subject, and the circle as the object, saying that the triangle, or man, was trying to catch, chase, trap, attack, harm, kill, or torture the woman. 8% of responses said that the man was trying to kiss or make love to the woman. Generally, the circle, or woman, was at risk from one of the men, while also being an object of desire for one or both men.

The narrative of male assailant, female victim, is perhaps an obvious one, due to a history of systemic male on female violence. However, it is worth noting that the participants in the study were not asked to ascribe the shapes human characteristics or motivations. They were asked what was happening, and almost conclusively they reverted to narratives that involved the risk of death, the promise of eroticism, or both. It is perhaps our unshakable fascination with these subjects, and how they coalesce, that is responsible for the success of True Crime.

[ ... ]

Lorrie Moore: 'It is only in narrative that we feel close to the importance and truth of something.'

[ ... ]

Georges Bataille – philosopher and champion of foot fetishists – is concerned with what he deems our fundamental discontinuity. 'Reproduction implies the existence of discontinuous beings,' he writes, in *Erotism: Death and Sensuality*. 'Beings which reproduce themselves are distinct from one another, and those reproduced are likewise distinct from each other, just as they are distinct from their parents. Each being is distinct from all others. His birth, his death, the events of his life may have an interest for others, but he alone is directly concerned in them. He is born alone. He dies alone. Between one being and another, there is a gulf, a discontinuity.'

'If you die,' he says, 'it is not my death. You and I are discontinuous beings.'

This discontinuity obsesses us. 'We yearn for our lost continuity. We find the state of affairs that binds us to our random and ephemeral individuality hard to bear.'

[ ... ]

For Bataille, the only true cure for this metaphysical chasm is death. Unfortunately, we are terrified of death. We want what death promises; that is, a return to a continuous state, but we fear the process by which we get there. The prospect of our own cessation is an appalling one, so we try to find ways around it. Bataille posits that historical practices of animal sacrifice were a means of trying to get closer to death, without having to undergo it. A photograph of a sheep, suspended and on the brink of sacrifice, has this caption: 'A violent death disrupts the creature's discontinuity; what remains, what the tense onlookers experience in the ensuing silence, is the continuity of all existence with which the victim is now one.' The sheep's countenance is benign and blithe, as though anticipating its imminent, posthumous homogeneity (it's somewhat redolent of that most Bovidae-looking angel, Paul Klee's 'Angelus Novus').

Sex, similarly, is another attempt to get closer, an attempt to simulate that fleeting moment of continuity from which we all stem – the instant the egg and the sperm fuse, but prior to their becoming a new entity, after which each former entity is lost. We strip naked and fondle one another in an attempt to reclaim that brief, glancing sense of having once been two entities on the cusp of becoming a new one. That sex cannot truly deliver this feeling is one of our great existential disappointments.

[ . . . ]

No personal testimony exists for the Isdal Woman. Her handwriting is preserved on several registration forms at several hotels, but she gave pseudonyms, false birthdays, false passport numbers. She was Claudia twice. Always Belgian. Under 'reason for travel' she wrote tourism; handling antiques; trades and business; a false German word that translates, meaninglessly, to 'trading with professions'. She wrote that she'd been in London, was going to Oslo. She'd been in Brussels, was going to Trondheim. As one podcast host puts it, 'This is a woman who got around.'

[ . . . ]

In the artists' impressions she is drawn as beautiful – initially, in the 70s, as a kind of Sophia Loren meets Jane Jetson figure, and then, in the more recent drawing, as not unlike Milla Jovovich. Her face is made to suit our desires. That there are no photographs of her (living) matters, because in this way one more aspect of her is brought under the jurisdiction of others. It helps that the raw material is good, that she is someone with the potential to invite intrigue and fixation. It matters that the strange woman with the strange death is sexy, to balance out the more aberrant elements of her personage: her taciturnity, redolent of an agenda. Her garlicky odour.

She's compelling not just for being incognito, but because she occupies some space where beauty and depravity meet. Perhaps, if the Isdal Woman's killers had been identified, they would now be the subject of media scrutiny. As it is, we're left with the victim, who exonerates us of impropriety by being odd enough – sexy enough – to elevate her above the status of a just sad story.

[ ⋯ ]

Explorations into the Isdal Woman's death are notable for their fixation
with her sexiness. Our cathexis seems contingent upon it. Lorrie Moore's
understanding of our propensity to narrativise is conducted in good faith – she
thinks we construct narratives in order to empathise. However, is True Crime
actually concerned with empathy? I wonder if the speculating, sleuthing, and
narrativising that occur through participation in this genre might not be more
akin to stringing a sheep by its hindquarters and slitting its throat: an attempt
to get closer to death without getting *too* close; an attempt to nuzzle against the
notion of continuity, without the terrifying, onerous chore of dying. The True
Crime genre makes it easy, takes the dirty work out of it – we don't need to
slaughter anything; we don't need to entertain, however briefly, the prospect
of masturbating in front of our mother's corpse, as Bataille did (although, if Mr.
Necrophilia Apologist is correct, such activity is actually akin to masturbating
in front of someone's microwave).

Safely ensconced within the serialised model of True Crime, the death in
question has already occurred; has occurred to someone sufficiently abstract
as to allow us to romp gainfully, guilelessly, guiltlessly through a simulacrum
of death's corridors. In assembling our own narratives of the victim's last
moments, we have a putative sense of closeness, whereby we bring the victim
under our dominion, and perhaps suspend, briefly, the oppressive thrum of our
singularity. That the individual in question can neither dispel nor corroborate,
question nor object, is vital. Our narrativising is permitted to go unfettered,
and therefore we feel even more like we might truly know them, like we have
assumed authority over their truth. That the act of making is so relentlessly
tethered to the language and limitations of our own experience, of our own
narrative proclivities, is a fact that is permitted to slip by, unchallenged.

[ 77 ]

[ ... ]

May Sarton, in her poem on the death of Virginia Woolf: 'I speak to you and meet my own life.' What does this mean? What should it mean?

[ ... ]

In obsessing over a death via True Crime, we trick ourselves into thinking we are getting closer to the aspirational continuity, which fascinates and terrifies. However, we need to ask just what the obsession brings about – is it a way to think about the porosity of the 'I', its innate vulnerability and susceptibility to loss and violence? Or is it absolving us of doing that work, via True Crime's provision of implied distance between the 'I' of the witness, and the 'she' of the victim. The ubiquitous sexualising and estrangement of victims is both a lean towards continuity and a step back from humanisation. If sex is an attempt to siphon some semblance of the feeling only death can bring, engaging with a death narrative that encourages us to flex our erotic muscles heightens this experience, but it also makes the victim undeserving of grief.

[ . . . ]

There is another consideration in all of this, and it stems from possibly the greatest flaw in Bataille's thinking – the question of individuation, of the integrous concept of the 'individual'. Bataille's theory of continuity holds implicitly within it the idea that, following the moment of our conception, we are free-standing individuals, resected and opaque. To some extent, this is true, but the ways in which it is untrue should lead us towards thinking about how True Crime packages death, how it ignores our responsibilities to one another, and how it frames grieving and victimhood: we need to think about True Crime within the context of the 'grievable' life, versus the 'ungrievable' one.

In *Precarious Life*, Judith Butler talks about the societal perception of violence perpetrated against those who have been strategically dehumanised by the military-industrial complex. 'If violence is done against those who are unreal,' Butler writes, 'then, from the perspective of violence, it fails to injure or negate those lives since those lives are already negated.' Butler writes about this idea in the context of 9/11 and the subsequent invasion of Iraq and Afghanistan. The American public was not permitted to criticise or question the retaliatory tactics of the US government; the American public was not permitted to grieve the lives lost as a result of these tactics. This is because the narrative around the invasion depended upon a clear delineation between 'us' and 'them'. To grieve the 'other' would be to challenge the membrane between the 'I' and the 'you', to question what lives are presented as real, and what lives are presented as unreal.

True Crime does not encourage grief, it encourages fetishistic interest, it cultivates our fascination with death, while also enabling an obsession devoid of empathy. As a single, deviant, unnameable woman, Isdal treads the line between 'like us' and 'unlike us' perfectly. The aberrant details of her personage are vital, because they allow True Crime to persist in its vaudeville approach to narrativising violence. By being nameless, by being faceless, by being unknown and aberrant, Isdal is easily denied grief – she is not quite real. Her death, however, is just real enough.

'Violence against those who are already not quite living, that is, living in a state of suspension between life and death, leaves a mark that is no mark.'

[ . . . ]

At some point Isdal becomes less interesting to me than the child who had to find her. She, her sister, and her father, are conspicuously absent from the information available, by their own choosing.

In *Jane: A Murder* (a complex, elegiac exploration into the murder of her aunt), Maggie Nelson notes that 'figment' sits alongside 'figling' (a little fig) in the dictionary. In *The Bell Jar*, Esther Greenwood sees her life as a fig tree, with each fig representing a different possibility for her future. In Nelson's book her focus is on its dictionary successor: figment, coming from '*fingere*, meaning *to form*'. It begins its etymological life as something notable for its shape, but by 1875 it has mutated to be notable for its falsity: '*We must not conceive that this logical figment ever had a real existence.*' Nelson follows this with a passage called 'Figment': 'I invent her, then, as a woman emerging from the sea.'

What would it mean to live your life, having discovered a dead body?

[ . . . ]

In *The Red Parts*, Nelson quotes from D.W. Winnicott: 'fear of breakdown is the fear of a breakdown that has already been experienced.'

However, in an article on *Fear of Breakdown*, Thomas H. Ogden says: 'It seems to me that for some reason Winnicott has mis-stated his main theme. What I think he means, and what he later says several times, is that the fear of breakdown is a fear of a breakdown that has *already happened*, but has *not yet been experienced.*'

[ . . . ]

I'm trying to think about trauma, and its lingering. About whether thinking of your pain as bespoke begets coping, or if some notion of universality could perhaps bring catharsis.

[ . . . ]

Maybe a new way towards continuity is not through sex, nor death, but through grief – through grieving those not known, through allowing grief to perforate the self.

'For if I am confounded by you, then you are already of me, and I am nowhere without you. I cannot muster the "we" except by finding the way in which I am tied to "you," by trying to translate but finding that my own language must break up and yield if I am to know you. You are what I gain through this disorientation and loss. This is how the human comes into being, again and again, as that which we have yet to know.'

[ ... ]

What did the girl who found her become? How could you become, following that?

I invent her, then, as a woman.

[ · · · ]

You know, I've never been to Norway.

# III – COMPOSITE

A plume of smoke dissolving,
Remaking itself, never still,
Never static, never lost

– May Sarton

## Prologue: You know that riddle about a river crossing

Say a man has a wolf and a goat and a cabbage,        or a wolf
and a sheep        and a cabbage,        or a fox and a chicken
        and some grain,        or a fox        and a goose
and some corn, or a wolf        and a pig
                                and some porridge.

The objective is to get all three across a lake in a boat that seats
two, accounting for the desires of each to eat        or be
eaten.

You can't decide if it's a riddle with a lesson: inconvenience begets
prosperity,        maybe; exert yourself
        to protect the weak,
        maybe.

And now you're thinking about something else:
                                the familiar image of someone holding
herself, making herself a barrier, between another person and a gruesome
or troubling scene. When this happens the someone doing the holding assumes
        responsibility, not just
for herself, for her own seeing, but for the other person's not        seeing.

Anyway. A girl has to get three items across a lake in a boat.
One is her having seen something, another is her sense
of responsibility for her sister's not        seeing. The third is what
she's seen: an image that will recur in her mind for the weeks
                                to come.

That her sister was so keen to see the gruesome, troubling scene was just,
invariably, the way things go (one's horror begets another's
curiosity), and poses

        a problem, because a person's capacity
for taking        and capacity       for giving aren't strangers. They share
a vessel, and their mutual exertion is maybe like adding more
      and more       ingredients to a soup already struggling
      against the confines
         of its container. So maybe the girl is the soup,
or maybe she's the container, or maybe she's the hand brought
without thought to the lip
of the pan (as if keeping scalding liquid at bay came at no
personal cost).
Regardless, the spilling over of excess ingredient is an image that will recur
in her mind for the weeks and years to come with rare

            abeyance.


All this is to say, the alleviation of your own suffering is rarely a byproduct
      of preventing someone else's, no matter what the Christians
might say. Perhaps the true byproduct is even
an exacerbation, because what you know, and will now always
know, could maybe,    just maybe,    be made easier by one person saying,
    You know,
        I know,
          too.


But the legitimacy of the image remains narratively unimpeachable,
because what detriment could there be in preventing another's
suffering? Especially if your own is *so*    unavoidable?

All this is to say,         a man had to get two daughters across a valley on
foot,
        without encountering a dead body,

or a man had to get three items across a lake, and two of those
        were his daughters. The third was the image
that would recur in his mind for the years and years to come.

And of course, there was no boat, there was no means to cross
        the lake, and the metaphor is struggling against the confines
        of its container,
                but there's a third consideration in adding ingredients
to aberrant soup and it's this: nobody is inured to the sight
        of a burnt body.

But I digress. A girl has to see something her sister doesn't
        – a burnt body in a valley – and now in the dark only one of them
sees the dark.

A girl has to get herself across a lake of silence to reach her father
                (the only person who's seen what she's seen),
and she does it, she makes it, but now his is the voice of someone
        who has endured
        too much, has nothing
        left, so she goes back to bed with the image,         recurring.


And of course, the real questions the riddle poses
are bigger. Like what kind of man is this that would group such incompatible
        beings? That would torch a woman's body and leave
the corpse

for a girl
to find? What man would orchestrate such enmity?

But wait – if the gruesome or troubling sight is a burnt body
what if *it's* the soup and

## 10: *Your ghosts were cowboys*

There's no such smell as burnt flesh. To get so named it would need to exist
independent of its visual. Some words have two protuberances, they're

antennae, half a weathervane. One frond extends to smell, one frond
to sight. Manure or vanilla or cinnamon have the right to live

their specific living (logocentric tuning forks). An example: your grandmother
is liquorice till you see her. Another example: burnt flesh is burnt till flesh.

In the moments before finding a body you were smelling an off-season
office barbecue or a three-teen campfire: cider and communal sweatshirt.

In the moments before finding a body you're young (about 10)
and you hope. In the moments after you're young (about 10) and you hope

nobody will ever take you to a valley and rob you semiotically, hurt you
like this. Once, your closed eyes meant the promise of Burt Lancaster,

generous in his lapels, impossible to know where stubble ended and shadow
from sun-rubbled adventures began. Now, they mean a woman's former

face. There wasn't a scream upon finding her, just lithic skin among
scree, tissue never seen preshrunk. This undisputed wind-beaten caryatid.

## 13: *For as long as you can remember, this has been a favourite feeling*

When a person's existence becomes known only on death
might it invalidate their prior livingness? Maybe. Or might it
reveal a new type of living topography – life as dot
with encircling matter, life as nebula, life as lake surface
onto which a big stone gets dropped.
Meeting someone at their close of life as yours
has barely started opening is perhaps like placing old bananas
next to new bananas; an empty bus sent to retrieve forgotten
passengers from a broken-down bus; your father underpaid
and anxious asking that you forgo dessert, and how
the dessert tastes when he says Actually you know what
have the dessert.
How to understand ageing as less symptom and more gradual
altering of ratio. From hot rain to cold wet on inner pane.
From mirth to mirth caveats. Maybe it's fine that your life
could be to someone else a sunflower doodle.
At autumn's induction you are ready for winter. For the stubby
wick's final immolation for the delicious life
-like brevity of days. There is maybe no homogeneity
of experience or maybe there is and if there is maybe it's this:
standing beneath September's last decent ripe sky
prior to its ceasing to be in season.

Vertiginous. All of everyone

inside you like a pale

black migraine.

## 19: *one problem lies in the fact that the word breakdown is being used in several different ways*

At the site of the breakdown there were hazards known
and unknown and the weighty promise of eventual response to hazard
lights. At the site of the breakdown you took taupe
and clotty stones from the roadside and put them in your pockets to weigh
yourself down while you waited. At the site of the breakdown you ducked
down and checked the digital clock. It was a small aurora in a palanquin
counting upwards to an unvanquishable uncertainty. At the site
of the breakdown you used waiting for better as a medium in which to feel
weighted. At the site of the breakdown you didn't get out of bed
for a fortnight and you emerged from the sight of the breakdown wet
-haired and kelp umbilical-d. At the site of the breakdown the brisk white
breaching of a Norwegian winter was like an episode of a scripted
comedy in which an elderly dowager snubs her family and bequeaths
her possessions to a longhaired cat.

## 23: We know little of the gorgeous sky's intentions

In July the world's lighting has commenced its peristaltic slide
to winter. The solstice is the world's cut off point for bone
density and the sky is spilt yolk on lilac silk, or catarrh on a pale
face split open, and the trees and houses are the flats and sharps
on the sky's etiolated keys. Everywhere are stark swatches
of monotheism. You wonder at the people inside who must
relinquish their bodies and nuance each night. Reduced to fungible
parts of this intransigent flatness. As the year barrels on
their moments as realised will shorten. Soon: November.
Now they have five hours at most for love or anger or hubris.
The little boy in the light this afternoon. His house is nothing,
as a Bok globule. You hope he doesn't get scared. You hope
he doesn't say, Must we be subsumed like this? and before
they're forced to once more stop you hope his mother doesn't stroke
his hair with an increasingly absent hand and say, Yes we must now shh.

## 24: *Time and size and moons*

The sun and moon were the same size to you once.
Two paintings in a café were the culprit
of erroneous thought. Moon and sun, happy
-faced as people or potatoes. Your father, angry
that you couldn't see the error. And the stars? Garnish.

Your view wears the paintings as you eat and your father
upbraids you. He's always approaching knowledge like time
is a circle, and it's true that something can seem
so obvious on first discovery it almost undoes the not
having known. That the moon and sun can't be the same

size. That having is invariably dependent on someone's not
having. Or something. The startling familiarity of shoelaces
and rain. But anyway. Maybe you said, and say, Maybe
the paintings' frames are different lenses. One magnifies
this much, the other that much. From here, you say, I can

sometimes hold the sun between my fingers. That's not
to say it's not large or frightening. Size is fallible as time.
You know better than anyone that a thing made small
by distance can nonetheless break you. To a listener-in
this conversation is happening for the first time.

## 26: There's been an unexpected change in surface volume

Suspect those who put cars in shopping centres. Then build.
Acclimatisation is the opposite of a doorstop. Calling someone dead
gorgeous is tautology. You're not the child who had your face
and if more big things were lemon-shaped would lemons come to be
considered small? Cook yourself a meal of sheer maintenance.

Oil the tray so the bits of meat don't stick and hurt dissenters
with a spatula. Watch a predictable acquiescence to the stimulus
of violence. Visitors will come to your home and say This is a dead giant
and you'll shrug as a never anything and say A dead giant what?

## 27: *Streamline first life then stream then line*

If the world were distilled to one of each thing
how easy it would be to love them all. To foster love
among them. Fellow – no longer concept recognisable –
would get melted down and made useful. A hinge
for door or imaginary friend for person. It's been so long
since blonde head was seen that person didn't think to think
of one when they colandered the noodle. In this new life of one
yesterday nothing is ageing but with one tomorrow
there is suddenly more pressure to die. The one-string harp
does its best for song and how lovely to never need climb
more than step for lake. There are no plethoras but oh,
such big grape. If it were you you'd take bike to meadow and wonder
why there was ever more than sun. If you ever get to old
you would like to look as though you didn't live yet when offered
suffering the texture of raisin you always say – yes.

## 29: *Dependence on the mean temperature of summer*

Nobody knows more closely time's vagaries than Norway.
Glacial epochs sandwiching a warm period resemblent to now

and weighing up the flora immigrating in the face of ice walls.
The strangeness of Bergen's mostly iceless coastal region speared

here and there with cute little glaciers and its Atlantic plant life
so much like you: insular in character. You find yourself moving most

in the damp. On nights when osmosis would only make the air
wetter and your eyes dryer you'll find reproductive prospects in bars

and you'll always abstain from taking their hands. Possessions end
up scattered around a bed like they're mourners at your burial.

Asplenium marinum and erica cinerea and scilla verna
and vicia orobus. How unethical seeking pain to exonerate your deep

unremarkable. Hunkered down in this erroneous boreal zone
– offered warmth and always recoiling. Seeping wet while outside

the cuticle holostea does its celery-convincing boney snaps.

## 30: *Thanks to a guild of urban beekeepers the bees of Oslo can safely fly across town*

Small ball cushion mosses. Unbelted eights with annealed
glass attachments. Shrunken fluff cufflinks. Since-dyed peripatetic
white mould. Inhospitable toothbrushes and so on.
One article says that bees shouldn't be able to fly
and a second article says this isn't true because bees can and do
fly all the time and sure that's fine but what about pegasuses?
It's spring where you are and a bout of bees
takes their unremarkable bodies pit-stopping.

A horse in theory would need a Sugar Loaf Jesus
wingspan to fly. A horse will never fly
to an audience a horse won't showboat or flex
for your benefit. There is mass scepticism at phenomena
not experienced but once experienced a miracle might as well
be a sandwich. You might have thought once that bees don't care
what people think but now you understand their all too sublunary
nature you can say with authority they do.
Nothing is more of this earth or its tediums
than you and you are not so unlike bee. You want to be
thought extraordinary and if not that then beautiful. Someone
to whom someone might say Darling how did you get here
         darling how are you hovering your wings are so little?

## 32: *A dream about two Claudias (or one woman named Claudia twice)*

partially after 'Les loisirs sur fond rouge' by Fernand Léger

Then red. Two cyclists in savoury costumes. One Claudia cracks
the picnic basket and peels a lamb's heart. The red. Sugar
all over the blanket and sugar on the hot skin on her olive thighs.
You can dissolve a lamb's heart in water and drink it like a Berocca;
sauté potatoes in it. The Claudias are sucking the open petals of its atria
like nectarines. Then red. The Claudias are a result of convergent
evolution. The possibility of a third Claudia is unknown but there are
peeled eyes in the basket and pâté and wine. White then red. Hard not
to be happy. They saw a dead fox on the way here. Tarmac then orange
then red. They toed it into one of the world's holes. Respectful.
Rode on. The sun has made their lycra hot and tight and wet
but there's always the promise of sucking granules from a sheep
child's innards. One more bite then home for a cigarette. (Deixis
and introjection dress in their wrestling leotards.)

One more bite then home then red.

## 36: *Fagus sylvatica*

But anyway, the thing is things are, or at least can
be, prone to cropping
up in places and times they're not supposed to.
Take the small beech wood above Bergen – two hundred
and eighty miles from another occurrence of beech
and erroneous with beech's true distribution.
In the 10th century Haakon the Good brought bishops
and priests to Norway with the intent of introducing
Christianity. This plan got abandoned in favour of remaking
a kingdom and soon he gave up making
the sign of the cross o'er his Odin cup. He ate horsemeat
and went crossless and couldn't get the sounds
to work. But anyway, if Christianity is thought of as species
invasive presumably Norway's riddled. It's eating the native
fauna and baptising the local flora.
At the time maybe he introduced something else, too:
a lowland plant with a usual height of not more than five hundred
and twenty-five feet above sea. A tree he befriended in England once.
But anyway, there are invasive
thoughts sometimes, cropping
up like recalcitrant beech. When death seems not so unlike
a contingency plan. There are mornings arriving
not sore, not sad, but full
of weather, or below sea level. Gripped so, so impassably
anhedonic. When these mornings come your response
is to contemplate a little forcibly introduced faith, some time
immune God against whom choicelessness might seem
like choice, who might turn minimalist living
to aspirational thing. A God who'd surely help more

than memory (what man introduced her
body to your landscape?), who'd surely help more
than the beech wood sitting idiosyncratically
a little north of you. What good could beech do
to your hopelessness? It's only young, after all. Geologically
speaking.

## 43: *Whenever you feel sad you enjoy the smooth refreshing taste of Diet Coke with Lemon*

The first person to climb a mountain did so intending to touch
the moon. A resounding biblical failure, but anyway.
This is what you will picture: meeting her later in a place where later's
no longer; your finding her resigned to an impeached past,
a time commensurate with a bus you once watched pass
with little consequence – having no desire to be
on it. All that is visible transitions into the retained
or not retained, but sometimes a glitch in functionality
means you still see so clearly the door of a house in a city you knew
you would never return to, but anyway. When it came time
to think about your obituary you could never get past the impulse
to talk about a door you saw once. Lemon-coloured and behind
which lay things you could never hope to know.
To follow a description of this door with But I digress
and you say this now, you say to this woman whose obliterated
body you found as a child you say But I digress, and in this timeless
nowhere she takes your hand and leads you to a shrub littered
with anatomically impossible fruits.
She says There are the things you see
that they don't see and there are the things you see
that they see and there are the things you don't see
that they see but wait: you don't get to know about those things.
You will look at the shrub and its impossible fruit.
Behind the door was maybe another door, as behind one trauma
another trauma. Behind each unscheduled beginning the need
for that very beginning and the fruit on this indelible shrub
               always yellow. Always yellow, always firkin-shaped.

## 56: Case opens [case reopens] 1970 [2016]

Nothing for days. [So, fast-forward.] Egg timer. [Tomato method.
Millennium.] On the walk to school count the petticoat fishing boats
on the perimeters. They are rampant and innumerable but count them
anyway. Count their cinnamon furies. At night picture a big circle
around the town in mountain rescue chalk. [Look online. A local man
with a metal detector says This is a good noise, to his metal detector.
He says When you're alone it's a creepy thing, to his metal detector.
The detector's equine neck is like a virgule with discovery
on one side and voluntary redundancy on the other.] Send half
your crew to the far north and the other half to the local millinery
to buy you a flattering and handsome searching hat. [Dig up clods
of earth and find the blue child's backpack run through with tree roots.
Notice its Medusa's headness. Hard to get anything done
with all these damn snakes, it says.] Look at the nacreous light
on the Svartediket. Look to the sun's aureus disco pants as a way
of telling the time. [Notice the growing no-light on the cold earth
like balsamic.] Make a restorative snack before heading back
to the lab. Tie a pink ribbon around the houses so as not to alarm
the people. Let their excitement die. [Remember their excitement dying.]
Let their amicable chat wither. [Contrive amicable chat.]
Plug the holes in your head with wet sheets to keep the spiders out.
[Plug the holes in your head with wet sheets to keep the spiders out.]

## Epilogue: You know that riddle (reopening)

Season of farrago plots and narratologies, of slippy
sky described as peach melba, of implied gesture and imagined
topography, falsified          noises.
          And you, your homodiegesis is what remains

in question. But you digress. You know that riddle
          about a river crossing?
The first time you heard it was from the educator who'd later
          make a pass at you, who'd say, You're so pretty, your hair's
                              so soft, but wait –

Oil droplets know best life, its movements, and so are
          life. Perhaps you is trompe l'oeil, not oil on a slide
under a microscope. Maybe it's I'll and I'd in a trench
coat, hiding in a cinema, eliding hard truths of soft
demarcations and permeable membranes, of the hustle
of syntactic veracity. You know that riddle about what an I
          can hold?

An I has to transport varying matters
of incompatibility across the pale grain
of a lake. There's myth of solipsism, threatening personal
accountability, but safe with the desire to shield an I
in another I. You know?          I know, and so – but wait –

The wall's giving up its adhesion. You've thrown everything at it
and the lesions are shining through, and the vessel is struggling
under the weight
of ambition.

Anyway. And so, you, I'll tell you – and this will come
as no surprise – *how universal* the things I bore

     seemed.
              But you can only hold so much, and so can I,
and so, I'll ask one last thing, and you, watching the winter
light scry through the musky proscenium between page
and eye, say: You – I – were – was –

cowardly. I – you – know – know – it's too late
for culpability. You – I – are – am – sorry, and so, forgive
     me.

Grubby hands press a soft consciousness
to the wall. Elsewhere, shame covers iniquity like a pink sky, like snow
over a valley, like yoghurt over the shredded skin of formerly tinned
peach.

Maybe you were frightened. Maybe you were alive.
               But I just wanted to say –

[ · · · ]

All of this is ultimately speculative. I hope most of it is wrong.

[ · · · ]

There is no homogeneity of response to pain but what if there were
and it was this: standing under September's last

ripe sky. All of life in us like a migraine and asking God, please be
kind, let things improve. You're as neither yours nor ours as anybody.

# WORKS REFERENCED IN ORDER OF APPEARANCE

David Griffith, *A Good War Is Hard to Find: The Art of Violence in America* (New York: Soft Skull Press, 2006)

Maggie Nelson, *The Art of Cruelty: A Reckoning* (New York: W.W. Norton, 2012)

Anne Michaels, *Fugitive Pieces* (London: Bloomsbury, 2009)

Claudia Rankine, *Don't Let Me Be Lonely* (London: Penguin, 2007)

Elisabeth Bronfen, *Over Her Dead Body* (Manchester: Manchester University Press, 1992)

Lorrie Moore, *See What Can Be Done* (London: Faber & Faber, 2018)

Ben Lerner, *The Topeka School* (London: Granta, 2019)

Edward Aronow, Kim Altman Weiss, and Marvin Reznikoff, *A Practical Guide to the Thematic Apperception Test* (Ann Arbor: Sheridan Books, 2001)

Fritz Heider and Marianna Simmel, 'An experimental study of apparent behavior' (1944). *The American Journal of Psychology* 57: 243–259.

Leonardo Da Vinci, quoted in Joseph Zubin, Leonard D. Eron and Florence Schumer, *An Experimental Approach to Projective Techniques* (New York: Wiley, 1965)

Georges Bataille, *Erotism* (New York: Walker, 1962)

May Sarton, 'Letter From Chicago', *The Land of Silence, and Other Poems* (New York: Rinehart & Company, 1953)

Judith Butler, *Precarious Life: The Powers of Mourning and Violence* (New York: Version, 2006)

Maggie Nelson, *Jane: A Murder* (New York: Soft Skull Press, 2005)

Sylvia Plath, *The Bell Jar* (London: Faber & Faber, 1963)

Thomas H. Ogden, 'Fear of Breakdown and the Unlived Life' (2014). *The International Journal of Psychoanalysis* 95: 205–223.

# ACKNOWLEDGEMENTS

I'm grateful to the editors of the publications where versions of these poems appeared: *The Poetry Review, Poetry London, Poetry Ireland Review, Magma, The Stinging Fly, Partisan Hotel*, and *Bath Magg*.

Massive thanks to my editor, Colette Bryce, for not only her patience and care with this book, but for supporting my poetry from the beginning. Thank you to the team at Picador for making me feel so supported. Thank you to Kat Aitken and Sophie Scard at United Agents, as always. Thank you to the poets who read this collection at various stages and offered invaluable insights: Kayo Chingonyi, Stephen Sexton, Gail McConnell, and Ali Lewis. Thank you to the poetry pals who offered feedback on individual poems and made them undeniably better: Jane Yeh, Alex MacDonald, Chrissie Williams, Martha Sprackland, and Mark Waldron. Thank you, also, to the Seamus Heaney Centre, Bookfinders, and the brilliant minds of Belfast, especially Tara McEvoy, Dane Holt, Michael Magee, Sacha White, Padraig Regan, Ellen Reay, and Scott McKendry.

I was never in any rush to put out a first collection, which will surprise anyone who knows me, as I have a propensity for recklessness when it comes to my own writing. This uncharacteristic patience was largely due to small press publishers, who helped me find my way towards a first collection by encouraging my experiments: Amy Acre and Jake Wild Hall at Bad Betty Press, who published *bloodthirsty for marriage*, and Stephen Connolly and Manuela Moser at The Lifeboat Press, who published the other three, and who will no doubt be coerced into publishing many more before I die.

Because of a convoluted psychological trap of my own making, I'm not allowed to thank my partner. He's been brilliant.

This book, ultimately, is for the Isdal Woman, a person I've spent many years thinking about. I'm glad the book ended up not being that much about her – it was the best I knew how to do.

.